Your Business God's Way

Author ~ Monica R. Philips

~Dedication~

I dedicate this book to my loving and supportive husband, Patrick H. Philips. Thank you for loving me and challenging me to be better each day. To my children, each one of you keeps me on my toes. Thank you for your constant encouragement to continue to push past my obstacles. Mom loves you, my FAV 5! To my parents, Mom and Pops I love you dearly and thank you for always being supportive. To my dad William Howard, I love you. To my best friend Beulah you are the bomb! The best friend and Big sister a girl could ever ask for. Last but not least, to every entrepreneur, I know the struggle, have lived the struggle and had to push the reset button. You can do it and you will succeed!

Table of Contents

1. Change your Mindset
2. Back to the basics
3. Seize the moment
4. Plan and Execute
5. Be Consistent
6. Get Organized
7. Being Sure
8. Watch what you give attention to
9. Integrity and excellence
10. Networking and Linking With Like Minded People
11. Remain Positive
12. Treat your business like a business
13. Fight to win
14. Know why you want it
15. Let go of the past
16. Team Work
17. Take care of you

1. Change your Mindset

We all have dreams and aspirations, and if you are reading this book, chances are that what once gave you joy and you couldn't wait to get up in the morning to do; Now appears to be stagnate. It's time to push the RESET button on your business. Pushing the "RESET" button requires a change of mind. If you don't change your mind you will be like a hamster on a wheel. Moving but going nowhere. So it's important to change your mindset. The way we think about ourselves and our business determines the outcome of our success.

God's word says in Romans 12:2 Be not conformed to this world, but be ye transformed by the renewing of your mind. Then you will be able to test and approve what God's will is. His good, Pleasing and perfect will. Being in His perfect will require you to change the way you think. Change the way you think about your current situation. Your current situation may look bleak and gloomy, but your right now isn't your final destination. Listen to what God's word says about your situation. Make up in your mind to change your mind. What you think about your business, is what will manifest in the natural. Proverbs 23:7 says, as a man thinks in his heart, so is he. If you speak positive things over your business you will begin to see positive results in your business.

If you speak negatively about your business you will get negative results in your business. Life and death are in the power of the tongue and those who love it will eat its fruit. (Proverbs 18:21) **Change your mind and you will change your life!**

2. Back to the Basics

(The power in your words)

This portion is a continuation of changing your mindset. This is equally important. We can curse our business or bless our business endeavors by what we say. Proverbs 18:20 says, from the fruit of their mouth a person's stomach is filled, with the harvest of their lips they are satisfied. You have to be very careful of what you speak concerning your business. God wants your business to prosper, so we must speak what HE says about our affairs. Continue to speak positive over your business even when it doesn't look like what you're speaking. What you're speaking will manifest.

I can remember when my childcare business wasn't operating at its best or at full capacity. We went from being fully staffed and at capacity, to having only 5 children in our facility for an entire year. I was so discouraged, but I refused to give up. I knew that God will provide. No matter what it looked like, I spoke positive words, God's word over my business. You not only have to speak it, but you must believe what you are speaking.

Remember that God's word says His Grace is Sufficient for you, for my power is made perfect in weakness. Therefore I will boast all the more gladly about my weaknesses so that Christ's power may rest on me. (2 Corinthians 12:9)

~Rest in God, trusting and knowing that even in the midst of a drought;   He is yet making streams in a dry place.~

~M.H.P.~

3. Seize the moment

Ephesians 2:10 God has made us what we are, and in our union with Christ Jesus he has created us for a life of good deeds, which he has already prepared for us to do.

God has given each of us something to do. Something special, something great and we are responsible for making sure it gets done. In Ephesians 2:10 tells us, God prepared us for what he called us to do. What will you do when the opportunity is given and the moment arises? Will you seize the moment or will you let it pass by as if it didn't present itself to you. God mad us who we are, and he knew what we were able and capable of doing. We have a mandate to walk in what God purposed for our lives.

Jeremiah 1:5 tells us that HE (God) knew us before he gave us life. WOW!! We were alive before we were "Alive".

Did you know that you are held accountable by God when you don't fulfill your purpose and you don't seize the opportunity? We often ask for the open door and breakthrough but never take it. Yet we continue to ask. Most of the time we look over the opportunity because of how God packaged it. Don't miss the moment by overlooking it with your natural eyes, but see it the way God sees it. Believe me you will know that it's from God.

~To live a fulfilled life we have to rid the excuses for why we aren't where we think we should be. No excuses for excuses! No matter how young or old you were born to make a difference. Seize the moment!

                                      Monica Philips

4. Plan and Execute

Proverbs 16:3 commit to the Lord whatever you do; he will establish your plans.

I want to start off by quoting a dear friend and mentor Shiketa Morgan, "If you fail to plan, you plan to fail." This is a statement that is not only true, but holds biblical principles. Part of our success in business, is properly planning and making sure we commit those plans to the Lord. Our plans could be awesome, but we need to apply God's word to it so that he can set them in order for us to attain the set plan. Many of us don't plan at all which is hurting our businesses. Part of planning is seeking God to find out what are his plans for you, your business and life in general.

Jeremiah 29:11 says, I know the plans I have for you declare the Lord, plans to prosper you and not harm you, and plans to give you a hope and a future. Our plans or ideas may be great m but God's plan gives us a guarantee. He promises us a hope and future.

So never just take your great ideas and just start doing something without committing it to God. Seek what his plans are and writing the vision and making it plain. (Habakkuk 2:2)

~Start today by writing down the plans for your business. Take them to God in prayer and speak life over it. Watch God establish your plans. ~

5. Be consistent

Hebrews 13:8 Jesus Christ is the same yesterday, today and forevermore.

What I love is how God remains consistent throughout the scriptures. He gives us a great example of how to be consistent in our lives. We know that in business things tend to change. The people that we market to, prices change, rules change and so much more. Even in the midst of the changes around us, God teaches us how to be consistent in our business, and purpose in life. Jesus was a prime example of consistency. He went from the crowd following him to the crowd wanting him dead. He knew that he had to stay focused and consistent to complete the task he was sent here for. In business many things will happen and many obstacles will come your way, but you must not give up and remain consistent in what we believe.

Matthew 5:37 tell us to let our yes be yes and our no be no. So don't bend or bow because of circumstances. Be consistent in trusting God.

Reflection:

In what ways haven't you been consistent in your business?

_____

_____

What can you do to change the inconsistency?

_____

_____

6. Get organized

1 Corinthians 14:40 But all things must be done decently and in order.

When your environment is cluttered, so are your thoughts and everything else. In order to see where you are and where you're going, you have to rid the clutter.

Something as simple as your desk not being organized can completely throw off your business day. When things don't have a place we tend to put them wherever there's an empty space. We need to take a look around our business and put things in its proper place. If you don't have a place for it then you need to evaluate whether you need it or not. While getting your business organized, our lives need to be organized and decluttered. That includes self-evaluation of the people you're connected too. If your thoughts and life isn't organized, neither will your business.

~Rid negative people, put things in its proper place and take the time to breathe.~

7. Being Sure

Ephesians 2:10 For we are his workmanship, created in Christ Jesus unto good works, which God hath before ordained that we should walk in them.

One of the things about resetting your business is being sure of whom you are and your purpose. You have to be confident in knowing that God created you to do what you do. Romans 12:2 tell us to not be conformed to this world but be transformed by the renewing of your mind. So don't waste your time trying to conform to what others want you to be, or trying to be like someone else. There is nothing wrong with admiring someone and how they run their business. There is nothing wrong with admiring even their style, but never try to be or duplicate someone else. There is only one you. Be confident in who you are and your divine purpose. Remember God chose you to be who you are and to do what you do before you were born. Always be a first rate version of yourself and not a second rate version of someone else. You were destined to succeed and to prosper in every area of your life.

~ Often imitated but can never be duplicated. ~

Monica Philips

8. Watch what you give attention to.

Proverbs 3:20 Keep Company with the wise and you will become wise.

If you make friends with stupid people, you will be ruined. Wow, this is pretty much self-explanatory. In business you have to beware of the company you keep and the things you give attention to. The people that you surround yourself with play a major role in the success of your business. Take the time to examine your circle and see if there are people that you are connected to that could be blocking your progress. You don't want to be connected to individuals that always speak negativity, who keeps up strife. 1 Corinthians 15:33 says that evil communication corrupts good manners. You become what you hang with. If you hang with messy people, you become a messy person. If you hang with successful people, guess what, you're going to be successful. The difference between the two groups is their mindset and the way they speak. So it's very important to watch your crowd. It is equally important to be careful of what you give attention to. What you give attention to the most will overtake you. If you focus on the negative or what your current situation is, it will never change. When you shift your focus to where you want your business to be and you work towards that goal.

You will see the results and the fruit of your labor. So be vigilant, speak life over your business and be watchful of your circle and what you give attention too.

9. Integrity and Excellency

Proverbs 10:9 Who ever walks in integrity walks securely, but he who makes his ways crooked will be found out.

In business it's best to do things right the first time. When you dint, it makes it that much harder to clean up what you didn't do right. In some cases you can't recover. When you can recover you don't make the same mistakes. For example it can be hard to keep up with paperwork and paying your taxes on time (quarterly for most). Well if that's not a strong area for you, then maybe you should hire an accountant to make sure those things are filed and paid. You don't want issues with the IRS or local government because you aren't filing paperwork on time. Another example is for those in the childcare industry, if you are licensed for children of a specific age group, for example 2yrs. Old – 12yrs old, stick to what the license is for. The BIBLE clearly states that when you walk in integrity, you walk securely because you don't have to worry about watching your back to see if the state is at the door. If you are a part of the body of Christ you really need to walk in integrity. You will be scrutinized severely and the first thing people will say, "I thought you were a Christian." Proverbs 20:7 say, the just man walketh in his integrity, his children are blessed after him. Our children are blessed when we operate in integrity. When we operate in integrity and your children go into business, because you were known for being crooked people will perceive your children for operating in that manner. So it's very important to operate with excellence and integrity because your name is on the line.

10. Networking and Linking With Like Minded People

Ecclesiastes 4:9 Two are better than one because they have a good return for their labor.

I love this scripture because it lets us know that we can't do what we do alone. In business it's very important that we network with like-minded people. Connect with someone who has already been where you are trying to go. Linking up with those who has been there and done that can help guide you in business and help you to avoid the pitfalls. Romans 14:19 tells us to pursue peace and for us to edify one another. With that being said, there is no reason for business owners to tear each other down. We really have to be careful of how we treat and handle each other; the very person that you tear down could be the very answer that God is sending to you. Reset your business by linking with like-minded people. Get-out and get to know who's in your neighborhood. Network with other businesses like the one you have. You only compete with yourself not with anyone else. Angel Alzono said, Surround yourself with like-minded people. Align yourself with people who think and dream like you. The old saying, "Birds of a feather flock together"; as cliché as it is, it holds great truth. If you hand with 9 broke people, chances are you'll be the 10th, and if you hang with 9 millionaires chances are you'll be the 10th millionaire. In order for you not to be broke busted and disgusted, remove the negative, toxic people out of your life and decide to grow.

Our business in life is not to get ahead of other's, but get ahead of our self. To break our own record, to outstrip our yesterday by our today.

~ Stewart B. Johnson~

11. Remain Positive

> There are people whose lives are tied up into your destiny. ~Tyler Perry

We know that in business we will face obstacles of many kinds, but its how you deal with those obstacles that get you through.

As an Entrepreneur I know firsthand what it's like to be in business and it's not going the way you think it should go, how discouraging it can be. I want to talk to you about remaining positive in business.

1. You have to intentional about being positive. The way that you respond to someone when saying good morning can make the difference in the outcome of your day. If someone asks you, "How's business going?" you should respond by saying "Business is absolutely amazing!" Even if you had 1 customer or 100 to walk through your doors, you speak as if you serviced thousands. If you're not enthusiastic about your business, who else will be excited about it? When you're not positive it shows in your performance.

It makes you drag throughout the day. It makes your day seem much longer. When you allow negativity to creep in it begins to affect your physical health as well as the overall health of your business.

Reflection:

Let's change how you're feeling. First and foremost find the positive in the situation. List 3 positive things about your business.

1._____

_____

2._____

_____

3._____

_____

Now list your top 3 things that you want to come to pass.

1._____

_____

2._____

_____

3._____

_____

I want you to begin to speak life and positive words over the six things that you have listed. Start thanking God for what you already have and thank Him for what you believe him for. Remember to be positive intentionally.

Thessalonians 5:16-18 ESV
Rejoice always, pray without ceasing, give thanks in all circumstances; for this is the will of God in Christ Jesus for you.

12. Treat your business like a business.

"Treat your business like a business and it will pay you like one... treat your business like a hobby and it will pay you like one."

Track your success, doing business when you feel like it will not pay you what you want to be paid. You should be tracking things like how many phone calls did you make, how many appointments did you set, how many presentations or tours did you do, how many enrollments did you get, etc. Be committed to your business. Set businesses hours and stick to them. Set rules and stick to it. Whatever you do, work at it with all your heart, as working for the Lord, not for human masters . . . . – Colossians 3:23 NIV

This is key in treating your business like a business. When you work it to the glory of God and not for yourself, God can move you higher in business, because you realize that what you have to offer came straight from God. Make the decision to be a business and to do business.

"Excuses are the nails used to build the house of failure." ~Unknown

13. Fight to win

Deuteronomy 20:4 For the LORD your God is the one who goes with you to fight for you against your enemies to give you victory."

The fight is already fixed and we've already won. So why are we fighting again? Who are we fighting? Most of the time we're fighting with our own selves. We must realize that we are winners and start believing in ourselves and the vision that God has given us. 1 Corinthians 9:24 tells us; Do you not know that in a race all the runners run, but only one receives the prize? So run that you may obtain it. Run to win. Remember the race isn't to the Swift nor to the strong but to the one that endure to the end. (Ecclesiastes 9:11)

Keep pushing until you see the vision fulfilled. Once it's fulfilled you don't stop there, you set another goal and work on fulfilling that. Press on toward the mark for the prize of the high calling which is in Christ Jesus. (Philippians 3:14)

Don't give up and don't give in you can do it! Take the limits off!

14. Know why you want it

I've come to understand that wanting something and knowing why you want it are 2 different things. You can know what you want but when you don't know why you want it, it can cause you to procrastinate. When you don't know why you want to succeed or reach a particular goal it puts you in a place to put the very thing that you want on the back burner. Then you forget what it is that you wanted in the first place. Not knowing what you want and why you want it will cause you to become indecisive about everything in your life. Here are a few things to consider when knowing what you want and why you want it; first you must ask God is this in your will for my life?

Proverbs 19:21 lets us know that Many are the plans in a person's heart, but it is the LORD's purpose that prevails. So go into prayer and seek God's purpose for your life. Just because it's a good idea, doesn't mean that it's for you to do. Once you know your purpose, take the necessary steps to fulfilling your purpose.

15. Let go of the past

Letting go of the past also plays an intricate part in the success of your business. It's a part of the mindset change. When you replay the past, you are not moving forward and the thing that you're focusing on has taken over and has ultimately become the center of attention and of importance in your life. Focusing on past hurt's, past failures, and old relationships can be detrimental to the success of your business and any new relationships that need to be formed. We miss out on great things because we often hold on to the past. Not letting go is like having an anchor that weighs you down and it prevents you from moving forward.

The famous words of Les Brown, if you want to keep getting the same results, keep doing the same thing. Make a conscience decision to let go of the past and to focus on the here and now.

**Let the joy of the Lord be your strength.
~Nehemiah 8:10**

16. Team work

A team is a group of individuals working together to achieve a goal. A group does not necessarily constitute a team.
~Business Dictionary~

This speaks volumes. In a lot of small businesses we see a lot of turnovers because they don't have the proper team. Teams usually have members who have skills that complement each other, magnifying the strengths and minimizing each other's weaknesses.

We can do nothing by ourselves. We can't be all things to all people. We have to learn to delegate duties. When you don't have a team, you run yourself into the ground. When you don't have the right team in place it's not healthy naturally, spiritually or for your business.

As I began to build my team in my company, I made a conscience decision to not hire employees but leaders. I wanted to reproduce myself and pull out of them what they didn't know was there. True leaders don't create follower's they create more leaders.

Make sure that you celebrate the team. Implement team building activities to keep the team motivated and on one accord. Steve Jobs said great things in business are never done by one person. There is no "I" in team.

TEAM: Together Everyone Achieves More!
   ~John Maxwell~

17. Take care of you

We have to be good stewards over everything that God entrusted us with including our bodies. As an entrepreneur it is easy for us to forget about taking care of ourselves, especially in the beginning stage of opening a new business. It's important to take time for yourself, journal about your journey and simply relax. Make it if utmost importance to take time for yourself. When you set time for yourself it reminds you and others that your needs are important as well. We must also take care of ourselves by watching what we eat and by exercising. When we are out of shape and not moving and just eating anything, our bodies begin to break down, we become sickly, it affects our mental health and physical health. When we neglect ourselves it sets off a chain reaction of events, which can lead to the death of yourself and your business.

Here are 5 ways to take care of you:

1. Get enough Rest- When you get the proper rest, you're able to function better throughout the day

2. Take a walk- Taking a walk outside not only helps you to clear your mind but is great exercise.

3. Journal- Journaling helps to clear your mind by putting your thoughts on paper. One of my favorite things to do is to write in my journal in the park or outside period.

4. Meditate- Meditation is very helpful and important to self-care. The best time to meditate is in the morning before getting your day started.
5. Make time to play- As crazy as this may sound, it's just as important. Ways for adults to play is to catch a movie, enjoy your family, or take a mini vacation or weekend getaway.
One of my favorite things to do when I'm not working is to Netflix Binge on a Saturday!

There are several other ways to take care of yourself and things that you like to do. So be sure to start by taking care of you for you, your family and business.

Reflection:

List 5 things that you enjoy doing and that you find relaxing. Then set time aside to do it.

1._____

2._____

3._____

4._____

5._____

Closing

I pray that this book has been insightful and of use to help you Reset your Business God's Way.

Prayer

I pray for every business owner that reads this book. I pray that each business is reset and prosperous. I pray that each business owner has a mindset change and that we consult you in all that we do. I pray for divine connections and favor for each business owner. We decree and declare that all things work together for our good and we will walk in purpose, on purpose. In Jesus name Amen.

Business Quotes and Scriptures to help you in business

Zechariah 4:10 NIV

"Do not despise these small beginnings, for the LORD rejoices to see the work begin, to see the plumb line in Zerubbabel's hand."

Matthew 21:22 NIV

"And whatever you ask in prayer, you will receive, if you have faith."

Isaiah 41:10 ESV

"Fear not, for I am with you; be not dismayed, for I am your God; I will strengthen you, I will help you, I will uphold you with my righteous right hand."

Jeremiah 29:11 (NIV)
For I know the plans I have for you, plans to prosper you and not to harm you, plans to give you hope and a future.

Psalm 5:3 (NIV)
In the morning, LORD, you hear my voice; in the morning, I lay my requests before you and wait expectantly.

Philippians 3:13-14 (NIV)
Brothers and sisters, I do not consider myself yet to have taken hold of it. But one thing I do: Forgetting what is behind and straining toward what is ahead, I press on toward the

goal to win the prize for which God has called me heavenward in Christ Jesus.

II Corinthians 12:9-11 (NIV)
But he said to me, my grace is sufficient for you, for my power is made perfect in weakness." Therefore, I will boast all the more gladly about my weaknesses, so that Christ's power may rest on me. That is why, for Christ's sake, I delight in weaknesses, in insults, in hardships, in persecutions, in difficulties. For when I am weak, then I am strong.

Psalm 23: 5-6 (KJV)
….Thou preparest a table before me in the presence of mine enemies: thou anointest my head with oil; my cup runneth over. Surely goodness and mercy shall follow me all the days of my life: and I will dwell in the house of the LORD forever.

Business Quotes to Motivate You

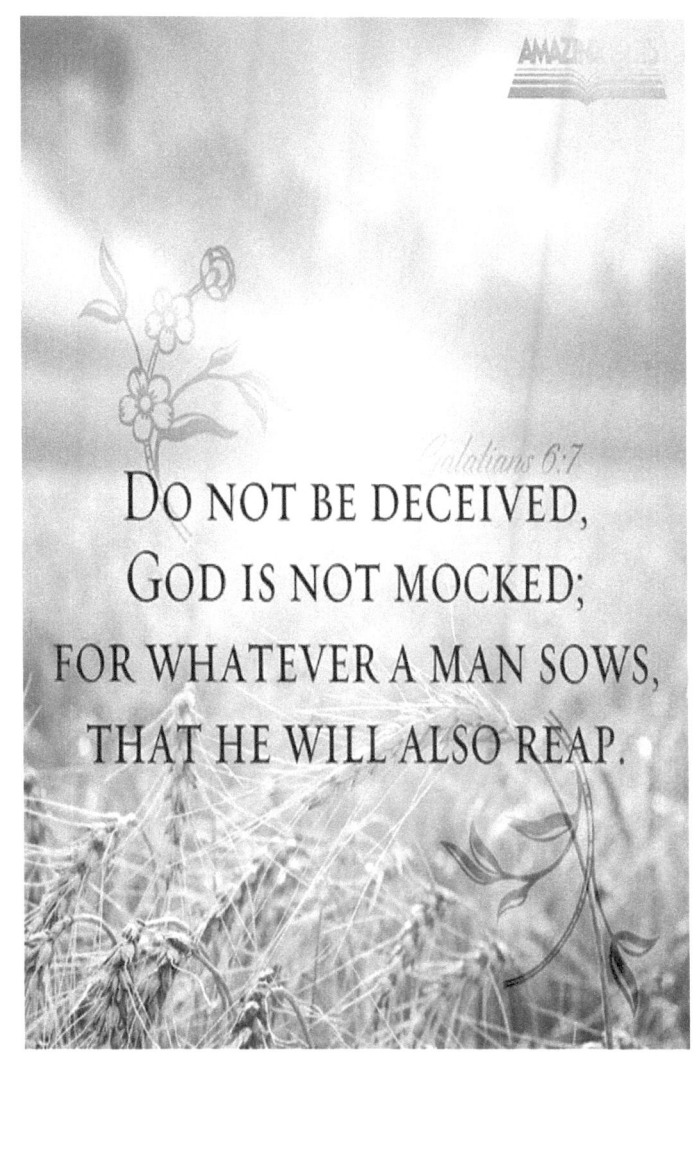

Sometimes Life takes you in a direction you never saw yourself going.. But it turns out to be the best road you have ever taken..

— Edzzzy Quotes

CONSISTENT ACTION CREATES CONSISTENT RESULTS
— CHRISTINE KANE

(G) Get
(R) Ready
(I) It's a
(N) New
(D) Day

"WINNERS FOCUS ON WINNING. LOSERS FOCUS ON WINNERS."
Eric Thomas
ADDICTED2SUCCESS.COM

> LEADERSHIP IS UNLOCKING PEOPLE'S POTENTIAL TO BECOME BETTER.
>
> — Bill Bradley, American Politician

> DO IT WITH PASSION OR NOT AT ALL.

AVERAGE WON'T CUT IT.

HERE'S THING ABOUT AVERAGE: IT'S AVERAGE. AND YOU? YOU'RE ANYTHING BUT. YOU'RE BUILT TO REACH HIGHER. **TO BE STRONGER. TO BE FASTER.** TO FEEL YOUR BEST AND STILL PUSH FOR BETTER. AVERAGE WILL ALWAYS BE OUT THERE, BUT AS PARTNERS, **WE CAN ALWAYS STAY ONE STEP AHEAD.**

Write the vision and make it plain.

The Bible says in Proverbs 29:18 King James Version (KJV)

¹⁸ Where there is no vision, the people perish: but he that keepeth the law, happy is he.

In this section you will write down the vision that God has given you for your business. Our words are seeds, we shall have whatever we say (Mark 11:23). Place it where you can see it daily and speak what you wrote at a minimum of 3 times a day. What happens is the more that you see and speak it; the more it will be imbedded in your spirit. You have to see it before you see it. Believe what you speak and trust God that what you speak and believe will manifest.

My God Given Vision

About the Author

Monica R. Philips is a mother of 5 amazing children and wife to Patrick H. Philips. She is the Assistant Pastor of New Living Ministries Apostolic Church in St. Louis Missouri, where Prophet Greg Roby is the Sr. Pastor. She is the owner of Little People Learning Center in St. Louis, Missouri and the owner of God's Little People Infant and Toddler Center also in Saint Louis, Missouri. Monica Philips is the owner of Linking With Like Minded People, a resource and coaching firm for Entrepreneur's. LWLMP host's a conference yearly for all entrepreneurs and business leaders.

Website

Linking With Like Minded People

monicadickens.wixsite.com/lwlmp

FB: https://m.me/LWLMP

Little People Learning Center

https://thelittlepeopledaycare.webs.com/

FB: @TheLittlePeopleLearningCenter

For booking email us at monicadickens@att.net

www.ingramcontent.com/pod-product-compliance
Lightning Source LLC
Chambersburg PA
CBHW031553210526
45464CB00003B/1292